CONSCIOUS RELATIONSHIP

Anatomy of The Human Fabric Trilogy

By Andrew R. Sadock

A comprehensive series of books designed to guide you through virtually any routine or extraordinary situation, to help you navigate any relationship, and to reveal your unique life purpose and life service through a time-proven, ancient prescription.

A HOLISTIC GUIDE FOR EVERYDAY LIVING
150 Essential Lessons

An easy-to-read reference book presenting practical guidance for gracefully navigating contemporary situations based upon ancient wisdom. A pragmatic adaptation of the renowned book of Chinese Taoist wisdom, the *Tao Te Ching*, complemented by other visionary, inspiring philosophies and the author's experience as a practitioner in the realm of holistic (mind-body) energy-work.

CONSCIOUS RELATIONSHIP

Using a simple analogy based upon ancient philosophy, this book answers the following questions: What is the higher purpose of relationship? Why do we attract whom we attract? What keeps a couple together in the long run? The book illuminates how various factors (natural timing, intention, communication, and the mechanisms of the subconscious mind) affect relationship.

VOICE OF THE SOUL
A Call to Action

A synopsis of personal transformation. Three types of activity innately unlock access to the wisdom of the soul—via dreams, intuitions, and synchronicity—revealing one's unique life purpose and life service.

CONSCIOUS RELATIONSHIP

Anatomy of the Human Fabric Trilogy, Volume Two

ANDREW R. SADOCK

Wisdom Moon Publishing
2013

CONSCIOUS RELATIONSHIP

Anatomy of the Human Fabric, Volume Two

Copyright © 2013 Wisdom Moon Publishing LLC

All rights reserved. Tous droits réservés.

No part of this work may be copied, reproduced, recorded, stored, or translated, in any form, or transmitted by any means electronic, mechanical, or other, whether by photocopy, fax, email, internet group postings, or otherwise, without written permission from the copyright holder, *except for brief quotations* in reviews for a magazine, journal, newspaper, broadcast, podcast, etc., or in scholarly or academic papers, *when quoted with a full citation to this work.*

Published by Wisdom Moon Publishing LLC
San Diego, CA, USA

Wisdom Moon™, the Wisdom Moon logo™, *Wisdom Moon Publishing*™, and *WMP*™ are trademarks of Wisdom Moon Publishing LLC.

www.WisdomMoonPublishing.com

ISBN 978-1-938459-26-9 (softcover, alk. paper)
ISBN 978-1-938459-29-0 (eBook)

LCCN 2013941331

DEDICATION

This trilogy is dedicated to my brother, Jonathan Robert Sadock.
Our time together, albeit too brief, continues to inspire my path.

I miss jamming on guitar and drums after school
and playing baseball with you, Johnny!
We had a lot of fun, eh?

Your sudden absence ripped me to pieces.
Then reassembled me molecule by molecule from the inside out.
But not without help from incredible teachers — whom I never sought.
Miraculously, somehow they found me. Thank God!
They taught mostly without words and led by example.
Guess I was deemed ready for them
as I'd landed in the sub-basement of existence.

I wish no one ever had to endure such an experience.
Yet this was the defining experience of my life.
All I do, all I think, all I say
is because of you and your path.
And, in turn, the teachers
who were graciously placed before me.

You taught me much. How to love. How to let go.
But only after learning the true nature of things.
That everything is impermanent.
That all situations are perfectly designed and timed
to help us evolve.

As my greatest teacher explained using words
but only after gifting me with a 5-hour transcendent journey,
a sacred inner trek which conveyed more than words could ever say:
"It's simply a 3-D movie. It's not real ... except to the ego. [Know that]
all conditions are perfect" as they are designed to help us transcend
ego/monkeymind.

Thank you.

My dear brother, may your journey be filled with Light.

Table of Contents

Anatomy of The Human Fabric Trilogy	ii
Dedication	v
Conscious Relationship	viii
Preamble	ix
A Traditional Definition of Love	x
A Functional (Helpful) Definition of Love	xii
Overview	xiii
Chapter One: The Nature of Relationship	1
Chapter Two: The Venus Fly Trap Analogy	3
Chapter Three: The Law of Attraction	21
Chapter Four: Transcendent Compatibility	33
Chapter Five: Common Archetypal Matching	36
Chapter Six: Longevity of Relationship	41
Chapter Seven: Couple Assessment	47
About the Author	55

Andrew R. Sadock

CONSCIOUS RELATIONSHIP

Anatomy of the Human Fabric, Volume Two

All relationships are imperfect — by design …

and thereby perfect!

For if relationships were perfect

we would learn nothing

about ourselves.

Without interaction with others

the unresolved aspects of our personality

would not be revealed

and subsequently healed.

* * *

Lessons are imminent.

They are a part of every relationship.

By design.

Lessons are the very reason for relationship.

The very gift of relationship.

Preamble

Nobel laureate physicist Richard Feynman observed that matter naturally attracts other matter, yet, paradoxically, this attraction shifts to repulsion beyond a certain point of closeness. The essence of this observation applies to all interpersonal relationships.

Beyond a certain point of intimacy, something happens in which the quest for intimacy consciously or subconsciously shifts to a quest for autonomy. Understanding this paradox and what may be done to transcend this challenge provides the key to a couple's lasting happiness, joy, and bliss.

Andrew R. Sadock

A Traditional Definition of Love

SINCE THE VERY BEGINNING OF TIME, philosophers, poets, artists, scientists, and certainly those actively engaged in the process of relationship have sought to define the true nature of *love*. However, to effectively define *anything* the concept under scrutiny must be broken down to its most fundamental components. This step is the source of great contention since love may be viewed as a feeling, an intention, a manner of speaking, an action, or may include all of these features.

Some say love is a feeling—a euphoric cacophony of elation. Some say the feeling of love is more than this, as though a combination of euphoric bliss mixed with the darkest of feelings when the experience of love bears qualities of uncertainty (and associated emotional reactivity in the form of fear, sadness, anger, worry, closed-heartedness, etc.).

Some say love is an intention. And that since it is underlying desire that creates the reality of love, in essence, that love is nothing more than this underlying intention—i.e., they hold that the desire to love is a more significant aspect of a valid definition of love than is the materialized form in which love manifests.

Some say that love is a way of speaking—as the spoken word holds both the creative power of intention coupled with outward expression.

Some say that love is an action, a way of being as expressed through outer conduct coupled with the creative power of intention.

And yet, some say that a complete definition of love contains elements of all the aforementioned definitions.

From a philosophic perspective, the experience of love entails features from each definition. Yet, *the important question is: how helpful are these definitions when the experience of love seems to go awry?* Does a definition of love as a feeling, an intention, a manner of speech, an action, or all of these, best help one, or a couple, to understand the core source of conflict between them and promote resolution and subsequent evolution and its inclusive serenity and joy?

Contemporary Western scientists proclaim that objects of love trigger "physiological homeostasis," bodily feelings of security — i.e, when "in love" we feel a physiological sense of safety based in part upon a perceived sense of certainty, a non-transient stability and security. The sense that all is well is transcribed physiologically by the endocrine system and other cellular systems.

When examined under a microscope, could it be that each of these definitions suffers from inherent limitations when relied upon as a guide to understanding dynamic conflict?

Andrew R. Sadock

A FUNCTIONAL (HELPFUL) DEFINITION OF LOVE

THE MOST HELPFUL DEFINITION OF LOVE for the purpose of helping you to navigate and resolve conflict in relationship is a definition that succinctly describes love as **the *action* of supporting another on their highest (most appropriate) path in every moment.** True love is *unselfish* as it considers the well-being of the entirety of the other. True love is *perpetual* as it considers the well-being of the other in every moment. And, paradoxically, true love is indirectly self-focused—as what is best for another is best for oneself in the long-run.

Integral to this definition is the truth that you may (completely) love another *only* if you (completely) love yourself. This means that your action toward another is truly loving *only* if you are concurrently acting in a loving way toward yourself. *Self-love comes first*—this is the foundation of a loving relationship.

Defining love as an *action* helps us to identify and understand the oftentimes hidden (or disguised) interpersonal dynamics that challenge the ebb and flow of any relationship—i.e., the reasons that relationships may not flow as easily and smoothly as we'd like.

This definition is a key to finding happiness, joy, and bliss—both individually and as a couple.

OVERVIEW

The three phases of relationship

INITIAL COMPATIBILITY
is the *bait* ...
The succulent qualities that consciously draw us
into relationship.

SHADOW COMPATIBILITY
The womb of lessons, self-awareness, and, thereby, evolution.
The aspect of relationship
wherein unresolved conscious and subconscious issues
are revealed
... and healed.

TRANSCENDENT COMPATIBILITY
is the outcome:
An enhanced capacity to love
(at human and universal levels)!

Chapter One

THE NATURE OF RELATIONSHIP

The Higher Purpose of Relationship

AT THE CORE OF ALL RELATIONSHIPS is a simple truth. Whether you believe it or not, could it be that the ultimate purpose of relationship is to provide a forum for learning about yourself (and, equally, for the other participant to the relationship to learn about themselves)? Are you open to the possibility that in order to learn most completely about your core self that it is necessary to engage others—in platonic and romantic relationships? The Ancients believed that relationship is the magnifying glass through which to see ourselves more clearly. Relationship is a primary mechanism through which we gain self-awareness. Recall that *the primary purpose for our existence on Earth, here, now, in most succinct terms, is to ... learn (a.k.a. to gain self awareness, to evolve).* End of story. Sorry if you were hoping for something a bit more glamorous.

Overview of the Mechanism of Interpersonal Dynamics

During the tenure of my holistic (energywork/bodywork/holistic consulting/coaching) practice, I observed that a common source of confusion in relationship stems from the conflict caused by the disparity of initial versus subsequent impressions of a potential mate/co-worker/friend/peer. Initially, we may view another person as "virtually perfect" (attractive, harmonious, etc.). For a while (approximately 90 days), we continue to attach to the idea that the person is almost perfect. We see the good in the person. As we spend more time with the person, we begin to build trust and ... expectation (attachment) based upon consistent behavior. We create the expectation that the person's behavior (and/or perception) will always mimic (be within the range of) what we've seen. But, alas, then comes the fateful day when Mr/s. Wonderful's behavior suddenly doesn't seem so wonderful or attractive. At first, we might be shocked by the "sudden" change in behavior or perception—as it seemingly came from nowhere. Pow! And yet, it was pre-ordained to occur at some juncture—by universal design. It wasn't a question of "if" it would happen but, rather, it was simply a question of "when." Why? The answer is steeped in paradox.

The great paradox
is that the sole purpose of any relationship
is to learn more about, and transform, ourselves.

The qualities that initially attract us to a potential mate are relatively superficial characteristics that may include outer beauty, intellect, wit, kindness, attractive style, etc.—traits and behavior that we find attractive. These qualities represent the succulent "nectar" (of the Venus Flytrap analogy as employed throughout this text) that draws us close to another person, and inspires us to stick around (intended pun) over time, especially during periods of conflict. Without the nectar—the overwhelming attractiveness of the other—we would run away at the first hint of unattractive behavior or conflict. And yet, the unattractive behavior—the "reactivity" of the other, as triggered by close relations, is essential for our, and for their, evolution. The higher purpose of relationship is to become self-aware through dynamics with others. The details of this mechanism are described in the following chapters.

Chapter Two

THE VENUS FLYTRAP ANALOGY
... AND HOW IT WORKS

INITIAL COMPATIBILITY
is the bait ...
The succulent qualities that consciously draw us
into relationship.

SHADOW COMPATIBILITY
The womb of lessons, self-awareness, and, thereby, evolution.
The aspect of relationship
wherein unresolved conscious and subconscious issues
are revealed
... and healed.

TRANSCENDENT COMPATIBILITY
is the outcome:
an enhanced capacity to love
(at human and universal levels)!

THE VENUS FLYTRAP is a unique plant that possesses powerful jaws that preclude escape for unsuspecting insects lured into the center orifice of the plant (a.k.a. the *"mouth"* of the plant) by succulent, irresistible nectar. Once the insect is inside the plant's *mouth*, the "jaws" of the plant shut, preventing escape by the insect (a.k.a. the plant's dinner).

The Venus Flytrap serves as an effective analogy through which to understand the mechanism (and higher purpose) of any relationship.

Metaphor: Entire Plant = Overall Interpersonal Dynamics

The Venus Flytrap plant represents the entirety of dynamics between you and another party to any platonic or romantic relationship. Two key mechanisms of the dynamics of relationship are represented by the *nectar* and the *jaws* of the plant.

Metaphor: Nectar = Attractive Qualities (a.k.a. Bait, Glue)

The colorful, aromatic, and succulent nectar of the plant—located just inside the mouth of the plant—is, initially, the irresistible bait that causes flying insects to approach the plant. Symbolically, the nectar represents those attributes we find attractive in a potential mate for romantic relationship and attributes we find attractive in a platonic relationship (such as friend, acquaintance, or associate). In the case of romantic relationship, the nectar represents the attractive magnetism of tangible (physicality and sexuality) and intangible beauty (mentality, emotionality, and spirituality). Initially, nectar is what brings romantic couples and platonic parties together. Later in the course of the relationship, after conflict has arisen, nectar is the glue that keeps the parties from simply running away.

The stickiness of the nectar (of the Venus Flytrap) represents the magnetic, attractive force of another person. The nectar is the force that hooks us, and keeps us hooked, to another person even when engaged in unpleasant conflict. The more attractive the qualities of another person—their perceived aesthetic beauty, intellect, caring (heart), strength, creativity, etc. —the greater the stickiness of the attraction. Why is stickiness helpful? Because when the "fit hits the shan" (when conflictive issues arise), rather than run away, the parties to the relationship will try to work things out—i.e., they will attempt to resolve the fundamental life lessons that must be resolved to preserve the integrity of the relationship—as they feel great attraction to the other person, but for the conflictive issue.

Nectar — Careful What You Ask For!

Of course we all prefer to attract a lover, boss, and friend who presents minimal conflict. We all prefer to attract great initial beauty and harmony. But, is there a down-side to manifesting great initial nectar (i.e., initial magnetic attraction)?

The paradox of nectar (attraction) follows. The stickier the nectar — the greater the degree of initial attraction — the greater the likelihood that subsequent conflictive issues with the individual (revealed after ninety-days of relatively continual communication) will also be equally intense. Why is this? Because natural order (a.k.a. the universe, God, etc.) gives us precisely what we need in any given moment — no more, no less. It gives us what we need on a less-is-more basis. It is precisely efficient and frugal. So, if we need a great quantity of initial attraction (bait), this infers that a great quantity of "glue" will be needed later — when great conflict/disharmony ensues.

In other words, the greater our initial attraction to the other person, from a physical, mental, emotional, and/or spiritual perspective, the greater the likelihood of more challenging lessons to be learned through that relationship. The more attractive person (from our perspective) is laced with greater probability to push our buttons at a very deep subconscious level. This is wonderful from a healing (spiritual/energetic) perspective, as this will accelerate our healing — yet from an ego perspective this might not be much fun (understatement!) due to subjective pain and suffering when our unresolved subconscious issues are triggered. So ... be careful what you ask for!

The 90-Day Rule

> At 90 days into any relationship,
> the "other" (unforeseen) side of the personality
> is revealed (by both parties)
> ... by design.

The Venus Flytrap analogy is most applicable when individuals are in continuous (and relatively "close") contact for approximately 90 days (three months — sometimes described as the "honeymoon" period).

Note that trust takes approximately 90 days to attain at a subconscious level. Close and continuous contact translates as maintenance of patterned communication wherein the intention of the relationship is to enhance understanding and synergy progressively. For example, new couples, newly-acquainted workers, family members and/or friends see or communicate with one another a few times per week, with the intention of eventually growing closer as a couple, working team, family member or friend, respectively. The 90-day rule specifies that something occurs at 90 days into any relationship — regardless whether romantic or platonic. Technically, at approximately 90 days into any continual relationship (again where there is an intention to grow closer), the shadow aspect of personality (ego) reveals itself from deep within the subconscious mind — as a reaction to the intention, words and/or actions of the other party to the relationship. This is the "other side" of the other individual's personality that we could not foresee. This may manifest as emotional reactivity in the form of anger, sadness, fear, worry, etc.

Perhaps you have experienced a similar pattern. Have you observed that the initial 90 days of any relationship tend to be joyous, lustful (in the case of romantic relationship), peaceful, and harmonious? Yet, have you ever observed a change in patterned dynamic roughly three months into any relationship, such as a sudden change in the mood of the other party (e.g., lover, boss, co-worker, family member, new friend)? Did the sudden change manifest as emotional reactivity in the form of anger, sadness, fear, or worry? Or running away (and/or blaming)? Or clinging? These are common examples of how others may react to us, and we to them — at 90 days into relationship, when the shadow aspect of the personality begins to reveal itself. Note that such triggered emotional reactivity is by universal design — it's a good (and essential) phenomena.

Why? Again, we evolve by unburying prior wounds buried deep in the recesses of the subconscious mind. The continual behavior of others to whom we relate, causes us to feel once more emotions (and energies) buried deep in the subconscious mind.

Hopefully, unlike before when we felt the emotion, we don't bury the emotion this time, but, rather, face it and resolve/release the emotion in a healthy, conscious manner. [See *Voice of the Soul: A Call to Action*.]

Why is it that we are not to know the (first-level of profound) mysteries of those we relate to for 90 days? Could it be that the reason we must wait is twofold? Is it so the glue of "beauty" has time to set, so we do not run away from relationship when difficult issues arise, and, primarily, so that we learn the profound lesson of patience?

Ancient understanding considered the lesson of patience to be among the three great virtues to be attained. Hence, mastery of the lesson of patience is a crucial step for your evolution. The *Tao Te Ching*, a Chinese book of profound wisdom, saw the other two great virtues to be simplicity and compassion.

What if we could manifest anything we desire, *immediately*? If so, we would not have the opportunity to learn the lesson of patience, as we would never need to be patient. So, by grand design, could it be that a 90-day incubation period is programmed into the grid of our collective psyche and, commensurately, programmed into our resultant material experience, even if for no other reason, to enable us to master the lesson of patience?

At a subconscious level, 90 days is the *minimum* incubation period required for *profound* (and lasting) transformation. For example, it takes (approximately) 90 days to achieve a modicum of profound healing while grieving a severed relationship. And, it takes 90 days to initially meld into a new situation (at work, relationship, friendship, etc.)

Metaphor: Jaws = Lessons Presented

Mastery of lessons
triggered by relating to others
is the higher purpose of relationship.

The nectar of the Venus Flytrap symbolizes the attractive bait that magnetically draws people together. Ultimately, if the attraction is strong enough, the nectar serves as the glue that helps to keep people together during difficult times—i.e., when challenging lessons prevail. For the initial 90 days of relationship, given consistent communication, the jaws of the plant, symbolizing forthcoming lessons, shut ever so slowly. This represents the initial seeding and eventual gestation of our triggered reactivity to the intention, words, and actions of the other party—which "push our buttons." At approximately 90 days, each party to the dynamic experiences at least a bit of emotional reactivity to perceived "contrary/resistant" intention, words, and action of the other party. Typically, such resistance (i.e., pre-conflict) is completely unforeseen—as though it were disguised and/or purposely hidden from view until ... wham, bam ... it's too late and the conflict engulfs you and the other person (mate/friend/boss/peer/family member). Suddenly and unexpectedly, "conflict" arises between the parties. Resolution of such conflict furthers our self-awareness and the self-awareness of the other party. Resolution may result in dissolution or strengthening of a relationship. This is of secondary importance when compared to the primary purpose of relationship—again, to gain self-awareness. What's most important is that each party evolves—i.e., gains self-awareness through interaction.

Only through subtly or not-so-subtly provoked reactivity—a triggered re-experience of previously buried emotions—can we fully evolve. Thus, thank those who cause you to experience challenging feelings: they are helping you to grow. In this sense, your greatest nemesis is your greatest teacher—as your nemesis here causes you to react, i.e., to feel unresolved emotions that to be healed must initially be revealed. In this manner, your nemesis accelerates your evolution as s/he triggers you to feel previously buried emotion(s).

Metaphor: The Insect

The insect symbolizes the naïve, innocent individual who becomes attracted to another individual, be it from a romantic or platonic perspective. The insect is baited by the beautiful nectar of the Venus Flytrap—only to become stuck in the succulent stickiness of the nectar which keeps the attention of the insect until the jaws of the Venus Flytrap close on the insect—barring escape. Symbolically, the insect in this analogy represents us when we fall for the initial beauty of another—whether romantic or platonic, and such attraction serves to hold us in the interpersonal dynamic for at least approximately ninety days, when not atypically the lessons to be learned in association with the other person, begin to reveal themselves. Thus, the insect is the individual who inadvertently (from a conscious perspective) yet subconsciously attracts appropriate lessons through association with another person.

The 90-Per-Cent Rule

This rule is another way of describing the "nectar" of an individual as perceived by the other participant in a relationship. Here, the 90 per cent of the person who drew us into relationship, their so-called nectar—is perceived as *wonderful* (or we would not have entered into the relationship in the first place).

One of the attractive elements of relationship is that the very act of maintaining (i.e., sustaining) a relationship—*whether or not it is a healthy connection*—promotes a sense of security ... which feels g-o-o-d! And, when relationship goes awry—we may be wary to release the relationship since, if we do let go, we lose the sense of security (which, again, feels g-o-o-d), which may result in feeling b-a-d.

Note: technically described, a sustained relationship inspires a bodily response known as physiological homeostasis—a somatic sense that all is well (safe, secure, and settled) based on a sense of certainty about the relationship. Whereas from an evolutionary perspective, physiological homeostasis may be reflected as a positive attribute, given that certainty in relationships may have assured survival of the species, in juxtaposition, from an existential perspective, physiological homeostasis may be understood as an illusory sense that is transcribed into the body—since there is no such thing as certainty, everything ultimately being impermanent (other than the Infinite Source).

Restated, physiological homeostasis is developed through sustained relationship,
whether or not the relationship is healthy.
And, as physiological homeostasis feels good,
we even hesitate to consider *letting go of an unhealthy relationship.*

So, rather than dig in, diagnosis, and then treat issues about the relationship, we may have a tendency to remind ourselves merely that our partner is wonderful and so ignore the key point *that it isn't the nectar of the other participant to the relationship that is relevant, on the contrary, it's the unhealed (less attractive) aspect of the other participant—and our unhealed aspect, and how our unwounded aspects engage (i.e., trigger and react) with regard to one another—that matters!* In other words—what determines whether or not a relationship is sustainable is not the nectar that brought the couple together but, rather, how the unhealed shadow aspects of the participants' personalities engage (trigger) one another.

Obviously, when engaged in a relationship that is less than healthy (that is unbalanced, ungrounded, not evolving, or, in the extreme, abusive or dangerous)—it is appropriate to examine the situation from an *objective* (or at least, *minimally subjective*) perspective. Unfortunately, this is easier said than done—in part due to the disincentive to separate—or even *consider* separation. After all, facing the truth that a relationship might not work out in the long-run, may immediately and profoundly diminish the sense of physiological homeostasis—resulting in an uncomfortable feeling ranging from subtle to gut-wrenching. I have observed cases in which clients as-though-suddenly recognize that their relationships might not be as wonderful as they thought upon first glance (or during the initial 90-day so-called "honeymoon period"). After all, it may not be surprising that their initial inclination is simply to point out what a wonderful partner they have, rather than believe that their relationships may have *issues*. This is a common attitude. Why? We don't want to let go of the buzz (favorable somatic feeling) caused by a sustained relationship. We may be caught by a sense that if we didn't perceive the person as mostly wonderful, then we would not have ever engaged in relationship with that person, or, more certainly, we would not have maintained a sustained relationship with the person. In fact, the 90% Rule describes the NECTAR of the person who attracted you into a relationship. So, of course 90% of the person is wonderful; the person obviously has some wonderful nectar that attracted us into relationship.

The challenge for us is to realize that although a person may be perceived as wonderful, our relationship with the "wonderful" person may be unhealthy, unbalanced, ungrounded, and problematically unevolved.

This rule was devised in response to numerous holistic healing sessions (energywork/bodywork/holistic consulting/coaching) in which clients expressed that regardless of substantial conflictive issues, they hoped to keep their relationships together—as their significant other was such a "great [guy or gal]." They unanimously expressed that although significant issues existed, they couldn't imagine leaving the relationship, as they still felt great attraction (physical, mental, emotional, and/or spiritual) to the other party. Note that in some cases the clients were enduring borderline emotional abuse or other very unhealthy, persistent conditions, yet repeatedly expressed reluctance to dissolve the union—again, as the other person was "such a good person" on so many levels.

These clients were *quite unwilling to consider* letting go of relationships, even where incompatibility (no chance of healthy, mutual resolution) had become obvious. They didn't want to let go. This stuck-in-the-poisonous nectar attitude was not allowing for any resolution of conflict. Here, letting go could open up the opportunity to ... learn about oneself (again, the primary purpose of relationship, even in the phase of leaving that relationship), and to do so in a non-dangerous environment.

As an example, I worked with a woman, Mary (not her actual name), whose knees had swollen to the size of grapefruits. She was virtually unable to walk. A holistic (energetic) diagnosis suggested that she was in an unhealthy situation with a man. In bodymind diagnosis, knee issues suggest that the body wants to "run" away from a relationship, but the ego stubbornly (i.e., fearfully) refuses to do so. I suggested they consider couple's therapy. She refused. A year later I was told that Mary was bedridden, unable to walk, as her knees had enlarged even more.

A few years later, I was told that Mary's knees were fine—that she was mobile and relatively happy. She had left the abusive relationship with her untreated alcoholic partner. Apparently she had had enough and somehow gained the faith that the universe would help her if she did the right thing (in this case, given that her mate was unwilling to resolve his drinking/abuse issues in therapy, the obvious prudent action was to take space from the relationship or, at least, to take shelter elsewhere until issues were mutually resolved). Initially she was afraid to leave him—as she described him as a "great guy ... but with a drinking problem." In time she gained the faith to trust the universe, given his refusal to engage in self-healing and therapy.

He was (and remains) for her 90 per cent wonderful—but the 10 per cent margin of unresolved internal conflict rendered their relationship futile beyond an initial period of learning. They no longer could bring one another supportive lessons. It was time for Mary to leave. And time for her partner, if need be, to "hit bottom"—so he would finally realize he must initiate a process of healing ... or live an unhealthy, empty life which would likely manifest in premature illness and, eventually, death. Note that Mary and her mate could, in theory, revisit the relationship, after an adequate period of time of mutual self-healing, if they so chose. For whatever reason, as a couple, they did not support one another's evolution. So, of course, the relationship fizzled—as supporting one another's growth is the sole purpose of relationship (and supporting one another's growth, in each moment, is tantamount to ... true love).

Letting Go

Of course, stereotypically, letting go of an unresolvable relationship—be it with a lover, boss, work peer, family member or friend—is not much fun, from the perspective of the ego. Yet, note that the soul regards letting go as a valuable lesson, when appropriate—i.e., not premature escapism. In fact, letting go is among the greatest lessons to be learned. Each of us is given the opportunity to master the lesson of surrender/letting go as we age. As we age we have many opportunities to master the lesson of loss. Paradoxically, if everything is impermanent (except the Absolute—i.e., God, the Buddha, Jesus, Mohammad, Allah, Krishna, etc.), such that—in the long-run—attachment is a futile exercise, then why attach at all? In other words, why do we spend the initial forty-two or so years [see "Timing" in *150 Essential Life Lessons*] of life progressively attaching to tangible things (spouse, children, house, car, career, etc.) and intangible ideas (information, beliefs, romantic attachment, friends—i.e., platonic attachment, etc.)? The answer is a paradox (of course!) ... we can only learn to let go (of attachment) if we have first attached to things and ideas. Otherwise there is nothing to let go.

Letting go may be described as "ego-death," as the ego clings to homeostasis, i.e., certainty—which doesn't exist (as all is impermanent—except the Absolute). So when ego experiences letting go of its attachment to a tangible thing or intangible idea, it experiences feelings associated with death and grieving (pain, fear, worry, sadness, etc.).

The 90-Per-Cent Rule and Faith

Ego holds zero faith. Soul holds infinite faith. Herein, faith is defined as innate understanding/knowledge/belief that the universe will give you precisely what you need, in each moment

... to evolve (as, again, we exist for the primary purpose of ... learning self-mastery).

The universe abhors a vacuum.

Translation: the universe will always give us exactly what we need, the "props of experience" (people, objects, and events that we interact with), when needed (when appropriate to learn a specific lesson), as these are requisite substrates of experience and subsequent mastery of life lessons. Faith acknowledges that appropriate relationships will always manifest—for otherwise we could not grow/evolve. We take one step to manifest an appropriate relationship, and the universe takes ten steps to support us—but only if the relationship is essential for our growth and self-mastery. The universe does its best to push away inappropriate relationships—by presenting signs via dreams, intuition, and synchronicity—but fortunately, and unfortunately, universal will may be overcome by personal will (leading to "tough" lessons that otherwise could have been averted).

The good news is that all situations and conditions are positive—as long as all experience is consciously observed and, thereby, viewed as an opportunity to learn.

Faith empowers us to understand and trust that the universe will always provide props of experience that support opportunities for learning self-mastery. Given faith, we can (relatively) comfortably let go of an incompatible (i.e., unresolvable) relationship—as we know that an appropriate person will come along ... to trigger our eventual evolution. I explained the concept of faith to clients, which helped them to find the courage to be willing to accept truth. Thereby they eventually became willing to objectively acknowledge issues with the understanding that the other person, although "90 percent" attractive—presented serious issues which could not be ignored for fear that acknowledgement might ultimately dissolve the relationship. They didn't understand that to truly love someone, you must be willing to let them go, and you must be willing to do what's best for yourself. With such courage, issues can be faced and resolved—culminating in enhanced self-awareness for both parties and, hopefully, the secondary benefit of a strengthened union with a significant other.

In sum, 90 per cent of any person we are attracted to is "wonderful," or we would not have initially been attracted to the person—but the 10 per cent margin, the reactive aspect of their (and our) personalities—is the dynamic aspect that matters most as this is the womb of the opportunity for mutual learning.

Conclusion

Note that relationship is not about trying to "fix" another (their behavior and thoughts) but, rather, the higher purpose of any interpersonal dynamic is to learn to identify our own dysfunctional, limited thoughts, words, and actions—so we can transcend (understand and release) such behavioral patterns. To accomplish this, catch yourself if you try to point the finger of blame at another. Rather, take complete responsibility for the situation you are in, for it was your choice to participate in the experience of triggered shadow personalities. Give your best effort to resolve issues with the other party. Yet be certain to exercise discernment whether to stick around to work through issues or to walk away (in the case of emotional and/or physical abuse, or when dealing with someone who persistently refuses to try to work through issues).

A Paradox regarding the proverbial Perfect Mate ("Soul Mate")

Paradoxically
if a perfectly-harmonious mate existed
and so never triggered us
to re-feel buried emotion and energies,
we would not evolve —
or would evolve ever-so slowly.
So,
is the perfectly-harmonious mate truly perfect for us?
Fortunately a perfectly-harmonious mate does not exist!

Of course we all consciously hope to find perfectly harmonious relationships (at a physical, mental, emotional, and/or spiritual level) — with a spouse, boss, peers, family members, and friends. We consciously seek flawless, eternal nectar ... without conflict (i.e., without the jaws of the Venus Flytrap — the lessons). Contrary to inferences encouraged throughout internet, copy, and televised media — featuring "perfect-looking" air-brushed models on magazine covers and similar distorting images and ideas, etc. — there is no perfect (i.e., perfectly harmonious) mate. A great paradox is that the subconscious always selects (magnetically attracts) the not-perfectly-harmonious perfect mate — that specific person who eventually will trigger the precise lessons we need most to resolve to support our evolution. We consciously seek individuals with greatest nectar (attraction) and minimal jaws (challenging lessons). Yet we subconsciously seek individuals who will accelerate our evolution. This is why the lessons an individual brings us — the jaws — are hidden from our conscious radar for 90 days ... so we don't immediately run away. Thus, a soul mate is that individual who brings lessons that further your evolution on your soul's journey.

Don't fall prey to the sensationalized external flawlessness being marketed throughout global media. It's not real. Nor is such perfection perfect. Paradoxically, perfect perfection is imperfect — as it does not afford an opportunity for evolution. Imperfection is perfect — as it supports our evolution. The soul mate, contrary to conscious hopes, is imperfect — which is perfect.

An Insect's Perspective of the Venus Flytrap Analogy

Suppose you are a fly, buzzing along, looking for food. Your favorite sustenance is nectar — the more colorful, aromatic, and succulent, the better. Suddenly, from afar you spy a beautiful plant (which symbolizes an attractive potential mate, platonic friend, co-worker, peer, etc.). You swoop in, completely focused with anticipation on the gorgeous nectar (representing physicality, sexuality, mentality, emotionality and/or spirituality), until you are very close to the plant, hovering just above the nectar. Even though you've heard some of your fly-friends talking about the dangers of Venus Flytraps (and other hazards such as infamous bug lights, spiders, and sticky-fly-strips) you decide to go for it—as you find the beautiful nectar to be irresistible. Caution thrown to the wind, you make a graceful landing on the plant and, with your little-fly-heart beating a bit more rapidly than usual, you have your first taste of the nectar—and it's even better than you imagined. In fact, it's the best nectar you've ever experienced!!! So, you dig in—and gobble up as much nectar as you can. After a while (approximately 90 days), having gorged yourself on nectar, you find that your appetite begins to diminish a bit—for two reasons. First, you have gorged yourself—so you've hit a natural saturation point. Second, after 90 days of feeding on nectar you begin to realize that although the nectar remains succulent and tasty, something isn't quite the same as before—you can't quite articulate it, yet something's definitely different than before. The once seemingly perfect situation is now less than perfect. The nectar-infatuation period has run its course. Is the nectar different than before? Perhaps not. Yet something's amiss. Time to fly away and return to regular fly-business.

If the Venus Flytrap plant didn't hide its jaws, and if its nectar wasn't absolutely succulent, the fly would not approach the plant. Analogously, we would run away from any potential associate who immediately exhibited conflict—rather than sticky attractive qualities.

So, ready for takeoff, you begin to flap your fly-wings, but alas, you find your landing gear is stuck in the stickiness of the succulent nectar. While focused on your fly-feet, you notice that a huge shadow is beginning to throw shade over you and the nectar. You look skyward and notice with utter disbelief that the two great leaves of the plant are quickly moving toward one another, obscuring your escape path to the sky above. Here comes the lesson triggered through association with the other person! You desperately try to free your fly-feet from the stickiness of the nectar, your attraction to the other. But, alas, you cannot. You are stuck in the nectar. Your attraction to the other person is so great that even in the face of unanticipated conflict you prefer not to run away with the hope of salvaging the relationship. Eventually, the jaws of the plant clamp shut; the lessons are upon you. You are trapped inside the plant, emotionally stuck in the conflictive relationship.

Symbolically, the only possibility for escape from the plant (the relationship) is to somehow gain greater understanding of how to deal with the stickiness of the nectar and the closed jaws of the plant.

In other words, you must gain mastery of the life lesson presented by your dynamic with the other person—to gain freedom, to evolve. In spite of attraction (see the 90-per-cent rule), you must attempt to resolve the conflict, within yourself and concurrently between you and the individual. Regardless of outcome of the relationship you must resolve your inner conflict. Save the relationship if you can—if the other person equally attempts to resolve inner issues and external conflict with you—or let it go. And have faith that natural order will present a subsequent association, which, similarly, will carry appropriate lessons.

Why is the Venus Flytrap Analogy Helpful?

The Venus Flytrap analogy provides an illustration that is simple, easy to imagine, and succinctly helps to see clearly the overall dynamic of any relationship in which you participate. **The Venus Flytrap analogy helps us to recognize fundamental truths regarding relationship easily, including**:

- **Lessons are a necessary part of all relationships**—as they serve to help us evolve. Every relationship has both nectar and jaws. The nectar is the initial attractive quality that draws us to another person. The jaws represent the lessons that always accompany the nectar (the beauty).

- **Paradox.** The greater the initial attraction, the greater the probability of an enhanced degree of conflict ... and of more powerful learning.

- **Profound lessons (the jaws of the Venus Flytrap) are slow to appear.** This allows nectar (attractive qualities that may take the form of physical beauty, intelligence, emotional connection, spiritual nature, etc.) the time it needs to work its magic — as over time (approximately 90 days) nectar serves to create a powerful bond between two parties to a relationship, sufficiently strong to discourage either participant from running away once challenging lessons begin to emerge. Profound lessons not atypically arise approximately 90 days into a relationship (whether platonic or romantic) — as trust takes approximately 90 days to attain at a subconscious level. Subconscious trust (at 90 days) encourages the subconscious to reveal its previously hidden unresolved shadow aspect, for the purpose of resolution (healing).

- **The primary purpose of relationship is to help us evolve by teaching us valuable lessons** — which are presented to us through our dynamic with another person.

- **The person that we are attracted to (or seemingly inadvertently connected to through circumstance) eventually serves as a trigger — instigating our emotional reactivity.** This reveals buried issues deeply rooted in the subconscious aspect of the mind — which can heal only if revealed — i.e., *felt*. This illustrates the profound value of the "trigger" (the other party to the relationship).

- **A perfect partner does not exist** — yet an imperfect partner or consecutive partners do exist — and this is perfect ... as we evolve only given imperfection.

- **Relationship is a privilege — whether platonic or romantic.** Relationship is a magnifying glass through which to learn who we are. Relationship is a mirror reflection of who we are. Relationship is among the greatest and most accelerated paths to evolution.

Anticipate the lessons. Embrace them wholeheartedly, with best intention. Work together to work through lessons, as proactive allies, rather than as reactive adversaries. If we know that lessons will most definitely arise, we will not be surprised when they arise, and this may help us to anticipate and thereby minimize the sting of emotional reactivity—which will help not merely ourselves but the other party to the relationship, as well.

Chapter Three

THE LAW OF ATTRACTION

THE LAW OF THE ATTRACTION OF OPPOSITES describes the pairing of platonic or romantic partners whose personality traits exhibit disparate qualities. Opposites attract, masking — whether consciously or unconsciously — their own deficiencies and insecurities. Each participant chooses a partner whose specific strengths compensate for their own specific weaknesses.

Manifesting from Woundedness (Why Opposites Attract)

The primary issue is not whether we should choose someone exactly like ourselves — as that person doesn't exist. Rather, the concern (issue) is that each party to a relationship may be relatively "incomplete" (physically, emotionally, mentally, and/or spiritually) and, rather than simply seek to resolve her/his own issues (i.e., weaknesses, insecurities, woundedness), s/he may seek another person who can provide a "quick fix" for uncomfortable feelings of inadequacy; this is accomplished by leaning on the qualities of another that s/he perceives as lacking in her/himself. Please note that there is nothing inherently wrong with this type of compensatory coupling, so long as each individual continues to evolve — and doesn't simply rest on the laurels (strengths) of the other partner. The goal is for each partner, through their interaction (and/or individually), to become relatively complete — i.e., emotionally, psychologically, and energetically resolved, and thereby relatively evolved.

A caution is that the pairing of opposites, if there is minimal mutual evolution, typically doesn't work well in the long-run as contempt between the partners may eventually arise. The "strong" partner may grow to resent the dependence of the "weak" partner. And/or the "weak" partner may grow to resent the control of the "strong" partner. Each partner will exhibit tendencies of relative "weakness" and "strength" with respect to one another. Things will not seem equal between the parties until each gains self-awareness and personal evolution.

Ironically, are seemingly opposite individuals engaged in relationship so different after all? No—first, each individual is incomplete (not self-realized). And, second, each partner is a gift to the other, as each shall help one another to evolve—through the ebb and flow of the lessons presented by the relationship.

The Mirror and Trigger

In accordance with the Law of Attraction, an individual shall invariably attract relationships that serve either to mirror or trigger their unresolved emotions. Why is this helpful? To heal (emotions), we must reveal and re-feel emotions buried deep in the subconscious aspect of the mind. Relationship serves to dig up buried emotions—for the express purpose of helping us to heal, gain self-awareness, and evolve. Again, this is the primary purpose of relationship. Two powerful healing mechanisms frequently occur in interpersonal dynamics—namely, mirroring and triggering. [Note that projection (transference), a spin-off of mirroring, may occur, rather than mirroring itself. This variation is discussed in detail below, starting with the section Projection (Pseudo-Mirror), later in this chapter.]

Generally, *mirroring* occurs when an individual subconsciously recognizes patterns in another's behavior that mimic one's own unresolved patterns. For example, suppose Fred has not resolved the cardinal emotion of anger. Fred may learn how to process (emote, react, release) anger better by viewing Wilma as she seethes with anger. Wilma's over-reactivity in her anger mirrors Fred's own over-reactivity and unresolved anger. Wilma serves as a clear illustration (mirror) to Fred, which helps Fred to learn to cope with his own anger. Wilma mirrors Fred's anger. Wilma is described as a mirror (of Fred's unresolved subconscious behavior).

Generally, *triggering* involves one person's innate ability to activate a reaction in another person. For example, Barney may become reactive to a certain behavior by Betty. Betty triggers a response by Barney. Betty is described as a trigger (of Barney's unresolved subconscious behavior).

The mirror and trigger are healing mechanisms that help unbury unresolved subconscious emotions. Again, to heal (and evolve) we must reveal (feel) emotion. There is no short-cut.

Through the millennia, and by numerous cultures, relationship has been described as one of the most powerful transformative tools available to help us evolve. Relationship is a magnifying glass — helping us to see who we truly are and thanks to the mirror and trigger, and also projection/transference — described below, starting with the section Projection (Pseudo-Mirror), later in this chapter — to evolve.

The Mirror — Theory

When Partner B's behavior mimics Partner A's unresolved behavioral patterns, Partner B serves as a mirror through which Partner A can see her own unresolved behavior. For example, Fred (Partner A) can recognize his unresolved subconscious anger (or any emotion) from a distance, when viewing Wilma's (Partner B) angry behavior. In effect, this affords Fred the opportunity to look in a mirror — to observe his unresolved emotional reactivity clearly. Wilma's behavior serves as both mirror and magnifying glass through which Fred can view his own behavior, helping Fred to become aware of his unresolved emotional patterns which otherwise are hidden deep in the bowels of the subconscious aspect of monkeymind (i.e., the ego or lower mind that views things from a superficial aspect). Thus, this helps Fred to gain self-awareness and evolve. Presumably Wilma also gains from the relationship — through mirroring and triggering (and projection) provided by Fred.

An Example of Mirroring

Consider the case in which Fred has anger issues; his default reaction is hair-trigger anger. The mechanism of mirroring allows Fred to witness his own behavior. Whenever he sees Wilma become angry, he sees his own unresolved behavior (his hair-trigger anger). She reflects his behavior back to him. He sees his own behavior as though reflected (and magnified) by his wife's actions. Hopefully, the observation of his wife's anger will help him to realize that his anger is inappropriate (and unhealthy). Perhaps this insight will inspire him to learn how to release the anger he carries buried in his subconscious mind.

The Trigger

Partner B serves as a trigger for Partner A's unresolved emotions when Partner B's behavior somehow causes Partner A to experience emotional discomfort, which is Partner A's feeling of the newly-surfaced unresolved emotions—which were previously buried deep in the subconscious mind. These newly-experienced emotions are brought to the surface by Partner A's perception of Partner B's behavior. To evolve, Partner A's previously hidden unresolved emotions must be revealed to be felt—and healed. Partner B's inadvertent triggering (unearthing) of Partner A's previously buried unresolved emotions serves to help Partner A finally to resolve these energies and, in so doing, gain self-awareness and evolve.

An Example of Triggering

Consider the case wherein Barney, who has repeatedly experienced prior bouts of a fear of abandonment, attracts Betty, who historically has experienced a repetitive pattern of a fear of engulfment (fear of intimacy). Betty's perceived need to run away when relational dynamics become intimate (primarily emotionally intimate—not necessarily sexually intimate) consequently exacerbates Barney's fear of abandonment, while, concurrently, Barney's fear of abandonment triggers Betty's fear of intimacy, due to Barney's attempts to cling to Betty to preclude her from running away. The fears in each individual eventually are magnified to such extent that they lead to a situation in which either or both parties cannot escape these uncomfortable feelings—and thereby must initiate a legitimate healing process to resolve these unpleasant emotions and emotion-based thoughts. In this way, triggering promotes a healing crisis—which helps the triggered party to resolve subconscious emotional/mental issues.

Projection (Pseudo-Mirror)

In cases of projection (a.k.a. transference), Partner A views the behavior of Partner B as a mirror of her own behavior—but unlike in the case of pure mirroring, inaccurately assumes that the intention underlying Partner B's action is identical to Partner A's intention—when engaged in similar patterns of behavior. In actuality, the action or words of Partner B may be created by dissimilar underlying intention than that held by Partner A when Partner A is engaged in similar activity. This causes Partner A to project her underlying intentions onto the (distortedly) perception and understanding of Partner B's action.

So, projection, a pseudo-mirror, consists of two components: partner B's doing something that partner A recognizes as also having done, and A's interpretation that B's action is done for the same reason that led A to do that action in the past, that the intentions for the two same actions are the same—when they are not.

An Example of Projection

For example, suppose that Desi and Lucy have dated for at least three months but are not yet committed to an exclusive relationship. Further, suppose that whenever Desi enters a bar that he fantasizes about meeting a "perfect" partner (who, of course, doesn't exist). Suppose that whenever Lucy enters a bar, she simply wants to meet friends—and does not fantasize about meeting a new partner. The result is that Desi, upon learning that Lucy plans to meet friends at a bar, may inappropriately suspect that Lucy will fantasize about meeting another partner when at the bar—inflaming Desi's insecurities. Unresolved issues buried in Desi's subconscious are dug up by Desi's worry about Lucy's intention (when in a bar)—as he has transferred his own intentions (to meet a perfect partner) onto Lucy's behavior. Even though Desi's assumption regarding Lucy's intention is incorrect, it is a pseudo-mirror of Desi's intention onto Lucy's actions; it serves to reveal Desi's wounds, and thereby affords the opportunity for enhanced healing, self-awareness, and evolution (again—we must reveal and feel—to heal emotion). Desi is afforded the opportunity to see clearly what his underlying intention looks like from afar. This creates a disquieting experience for Desi and thereby serves as a platform for internal change and profound transformation.

Unresolved Parental Dynamics

Triggering, mirroring, and projection tend to stir the seeds of unresolved emotions planted by childhood dynamics (and, according to some ancient cultures, karma). We attract the persons who trigger, mirror, and/or project upon us, for the purpose of digging up subconscious stagnant emotional/mental energies—so we can heal and evolve. We continue to attract these individuals into our lives until we have healed internally. Once a specific issue is healed within us, we need not attract others to unearth the subconscious (regarding this specific issue).

For example, consider the case of an individual who wasn't able to resolve completely her dynamic with an alcoholic father (who demonstrated poor anger management; note that alcoholism and anger issues oftentimes accompany one another—as both issues affect the liver). The Law of Attraction dictates that the daughter may subconsciously attract a relationship with another alcoholic (who exhibits reactive anger)—to afford her another opportunity to resolve wounds instilled during childhood through the dynamic with her father.

This pattern of attraction will repeat until her unresolved wounds are healed; she may attract additional alcoholics (or people with anger management issues) until she resolves whatever issues the interaction with alcoholics (and people holding anger management issues) trigger in her.

Healing Crisis

The objective of triggering, mirroring, and projecting is to force a crisis ("healing crisis") whereby an individual gains recognition that there is no alternative but to change. At this uncomfortable juncture, the individual finally recognizes that more of the same action will lead only to a similar, unpalatable, uncomfortable result. This is the point of profound realization—realization that change via profound healing is the only viable option.

From the perspective of the soul, a healing crisis is a gift—for although the healing process may result in some temporary discomfort and requisite sacrifice (letting go of what no longer serves us), a healing crisis inevitably leads us to higher ground. In contrast, the near-sighted ego views healing crises merely as uncomfortable experiences (to be avoided, if possible).

Pre-scheduled inner crises are programmed into psyche at specific ages, by design, to assure personal growth. These crises occur every seven years (at specific ages of chakra development). [These stages are discussed in detail in *Voice of the Soul: A Call to Action*.]

The Functional Definition of Love (Reprise)

Again, to love another completely is to support that person on his/her highest path, in all moments, to support the evolution and self-awareness of the other in whatever manner is most appropriate—in self-less acts may seem like compromise in the short-term, yet in the long-term provide equal gain to both.

Paradoxically
we can act
in an unconditionally loving manner
toward another
only if we have learned
how to love ourselves fully.

Love Thyself

To love another completely—to *act* in a loving way to another completely—one must first learn to love oneself. One must live in alignment with the dictates of one's soul. The soul knows who we are. We must practice soul-aligned activity—activity that aligns us with our true nature—including our life purpose and life service. Such activity includes self-nurturing, self-care, living passionately by practicing core creativity, staying connected to highest consciousness, releasing emotional/mental subconscious and conscious stagnant energies, and taking responsibility for all thought, word, and action—in every moment. For only then are we profoundly clear in mind and body. Only then are we fully connected to soul—and thereby able to understand the needs of another. And able to support the needs of another, even when different from our own needs and desires. All we are is what we focus upon in the moment. For all that exists is this moment. And this moment. And this moment. So, to love ourselves means to practice soul-aligned (conscious) activity in each moment. In this moment. In this moment. And in this moment.

Loving actions are activities that serve to raise one's self-awareness. Only given self-awareness can we profoundly help another to receive love and enhanced self-understanding. We can only bring someone as far as we have traveled. So we must do our work, to enhance (love) ourselves, to love others.

Phase 1
Initial-Compatibility: Nectar of the Venus Flytrap

Couples initially connect on four essential levels. Interpersonal dynamics tread the physical, emotional, intellectual, and spiritual planes. Obviously, superficial compatibility between two people may be detected relatively quickly. It is analogous to the nectar, the irresistible attraction, of the Venus Fly Trap without which both the immediate and sustained interplay of individuals would not occur. The value of initial-compatibility is measured by its "stickiness"—i.e., whether it is strong enough to keep a couple together when difficult issues arise.

Phase 2
Shadow-Compatibility: Measure of a "Healthy" Couple

Theoretically, a couple with a minimal degree of initial-compatibility may relate to one another in a loving way, on a long-term basis, if they learn how to develop shadow-compatibility. A shadow-compatible couple is able to work through inevitable differences in a graceful and loving manner.

Shadow-compatibility is defined as a level of *cooperation* that is maintained when confronted with subconscious and conscious emotional and mental divergence, and resultant mutual reactivity, between parties to a relationship.

Disagreements are inevitable (especially during preliminary stages of evolution)—by design. No two people interpret every situation in the same way—and so friction ensues. In practical terms, without life's friction we would not evolve. We would not have opportunities to learn (experientially integrate) certain fundamental life lessons (regarding interpersonal dynamics). We would not become self-aware. And so, the issue is not whether disagreements will arise. They will. Again and again. By design. *The issue is how we deal with disagreement* (divergent opinions) and interpersonal dynamics.

Disparity between parties to relationships typically stems from unresolved, subconscious emotional/mental wounds. These wounds hide deep within the shadow aspect of the subconscious mind. Not atypically, the shadow aspect of personality is revealed at approximately 90 days into a (close) relationship. This is when we begin to see the "other side" of the person (that we did not anticipate). Quite often we are surprised, if not shocked, to learn that the person exhibits certain unforeseen unattractive traits (and beliefs). By design, the shadow aspect of each individual triggers, mirrors, or projects upon the shadow aspect of one another—causing conflict. Again, the issue is not whether conflict will arise. It will by design. The issue is how we deal with conflict with another person.

Unlike a shadow-*incompatible* couple who take adversarial positions when in the grips of conflict, a shadow-*compatible* couple is able to maintain heightened awareness of the truth of the situation. The shadow-compatible couple recognizes that conflict will inevitably occur. They recognize that any emotional and/or mental reactivity by the other person or themselves is merely the necessary un-burying of the shadow aspect of the personality, the ego—a helpful and necessary mechanism by which to heal and evolve. And so, when conflict ensues, the shadow-compatible parties do not play the blame game or attack one another. Rather, they recognize—preferably through open dialogue—that one or both of the parties is merely "reacting" to triggering by, mirroring by, and/or projection upon, the other party. They do not take adversarial positions. They realize that they are a team, helping one another to evolve through their interpersonal dynamic, regardless how challenging it may be.

The shadow-compatible parties elevate their focus from the level of the monkeymind to higher mind awareness. When faced with a conflictive situation, each participant first recognizes and takes responsibility for their contribution to the conflict—rather than pointing fingers of blame at one another. The shadow-compatible couple maintains a loving demeanor when in the throes of conflict, rather than assuming adversarial positions. A shadow-conscious couple is not emotionally reactive—as their degree of self-awareness maintains focused in the higher mind, rather than monkeymind.

Rather than resent and confront a partner when unresolved, unconscious emotions rear their not-so-pretty heads, the aware individual maintains an open-heart and is mindful of compassion for the perspective and discomfort of the other. The aware, shadow-compatible couple proactively anticipates speed bumps (conflict) and greater challenges on the road of relationship. The shadow-compatible couple is certain to remember in each moment that no one is perfect, as we all have baggage, and at some juncture (usually after approximately 90 days) that any two individuals engaged in intimate relationship will trigger, mirror, and project upon one another. By design. They remind themselves that this is a natural aspect of relationship.

The shadow-compatible couple is aware that conflict can bring a couple closer together (enhance intimacy and trust), if handled in an appropriate, conscious manner. And that resolution of conflict can enhance the self-awareness of each individual. Mutual trust is enhanced as the couple, together, master lessons that trigger, mirror, and project upon one another. Rather than view disagreement with contempt, they embrace the opportunity to grow as a couple.

When unresolved emotions arise, each party in the shadow-compatible couple makes a conscious choice (in each moment) to maintain a higher perspective that refuses to experience (and process information) from the truncated perspective of the wounded "inner child." The couple maintains an allied stance while analyzing the conflict—rather than taking adversarial positions. The shadow-compatible parties progressively transcend lessons of enhanced profound nature. With each round of successful resolution, the couple gains mutual trust. The couple grows individually as well as collectively.

Shadow-Compatibility Trumps Initial-Compatibility

Shadow-compatibility
not initial-compatibility
determines the longevity
of a couple.

Shadow-compatibility, not initial-compatibility, is the feature that dictates the longevity of a couple. A fundamental measure of the relative health of a couple is the couple's ability to work through their differences ... gracefully—as allies, rather than as adversaries. No matter how compatible two individuals may be at the beginning of a relationship (on physical, chemical, emotional, intellectual, and spiritual levels), without shadow-compatibility the couple will not achieve its higher purpose of individual and collective evolution (through enhanced self-

awareness). *The shadow-compatible couple maintains awareness that enhanced self-realization is the ultimate goal of relationship. They maintain awareness in each moment that the mastery of lessons inspired by triggering, mirroring, and projection is the reason for coupling, so they embrace disagreements not as mutual pains-in-the-ass to be avoided at all costs but, rather, as opportunities for self-growth and the possibility of enhanced mutual trust and longevity of relationship, if appropriate.*

Chapter Four

TRANSCENDENT COMPATIBILITY

Third and Final Phase

TRANSCENDENT COMPATIBILITY
is the outcome:
an enhanced capacity to love

SUCCINCTLY STATED, transcendent compatibility is the third (of three) aspect(s) of the conscious relationship. Here, the three phases of relationship are initial compatibility, shadow compatibility, and transcendent compatibility.

As described earlier, initial compatibility is the nectar that brings and holds the parties to a relationship together (on an emotional/psychenergetic level). This is the perceived attractiveness of the other person. In a romantic, business, friendship, and acquaintanceship, a person's physical, emotional, intellectual, and/or spiritual nature may draw us to become emotionally/psychenergetically connected to them — a process that ensues for approximately 90 days.

Then, at approximately 90 days into a relationship, a natural process begins wherein the parties to the relationship subtly or not-so-subtly may become emotionally reactive in response to the cues of the other. In technical terms, the shadow aspect of the egoic personality reveals itself (from the depths of the subconscious mind). Note that this is the primary purpose of relationship — to dig up buried emotional/psychenergetic gunk, i.e., one's unresolved issues. Recall that *"to heal we must reveal"* (*i.e.*, un-bury) unresolved issues (i.e., wounds).

As described earlier, this is the very purpose of relationship — to serve as a magnifying glass beneath which unresolved emotions/psychenergies reveal themselves ... so we can resolve these energies (i.e., heal) and thereby evolve! Again, this is *the* reason for relationship.

Shadow compatibility is the process of mutually gaining self-awareness such that both parties to the relationship—together and individually—resolve their freshly revealed (i.e., un-buried) issues, i.e., emotional reactivities, that were dug up by the mechanism of relationship. Shadow compatibility eventually may develop, given that there is emotional/psychenergetic work happening for the two both as a couple and individually.

The third and final phase of relationship, transcendent compatibility, does not necessarily occur in sequence (following initial compatibility and shadow compatibility), yet it occurs in purest form when following shadow compatibility. Transcendent compatibility is the *manifested capacity to love purely*.

Recall that a functional definition of *love* is the supporting of the other on that persons's highest path. To do so, to purely love, we must purely love ourselves. And, paradoxically, we must be able also to focus purely upon the highest path of the other.

The phase of initial compatibility consciously and, arguably, more so subconsciously, draws us closer and closer to another person—who holds a key to our evolution (a.k.a. self-healing), as te other has the unique ability to trigger us (both consciously and, again more so, subconsciously) so we can innately unbury unresolved emotion and psychenergies from the depths of the subconscious mind.

This process, the protocol of shadow compatibility, is a fundamental mechanism through which we may heal buried emotion ... and evolve (gain self-awareness). *From the perspective of ego, the process of shadow compatibility seems like a trap—it's the grunt work of relationship ... not fun ... yet essential to our evolution.* The process of shadow compatibility releases us from hair-trigger emotional reactivity, as it releases unresolved emotional patterns. The clouds of interpersonal reactivity dispelled, we can now more fully love ourselves — and another. We can now more effortlessly engage in Transcendent Compatibility, the act of supporting another on their highest path.

Chapter Five

COMMON ARCHETYPAL MATCHING

WE SUBCONSCIOUSLY MANIFEST a mate/partner/peer from the magnetic radiance emanating from the energetic template of our unresolved issues, our wounded shadow aspect buried deep in the subconscious mind. To heal and evolve we must reveal and feel buried stagnant emotions and thoughts. To dig up prior feelings that we were not ready to deal with appropriately — we consequently buried the emotions and thoughts — we manifest connection to another person whose shadow will trigger, mirror, or project upon our own shadow aspect in a way that has us react from the depth of the shadow aspect of the subconscious mind. If we do not reveal and experience clearly buried "stuck" emotions and thoughts, we continue to repeat difficult lessons — without resolution.

To help us evolve, the following types of pairings support core healing in each party to a dynamic.

Before I list the archetype pairings, note that each personality has a conscious and subconscious aspect. And, the shadow aspect of the personality swings to both sides of any issue like a pendulum (as the ego is unbalanced).

Thus, a person who exhibits the fear of abandonment archetype predominantly expresses fear of abandonment — as this is the primary conscious fear, yet also expresses fear of engulfment — the opposite of fear of abandonment at the subconscious level.

This is why the game of "cat and mouse" occurs in relationship wherein one person may chase as the other seems to run away, only to flip to opposite reactions, and then flip back to the original "cat and mouse" dynamic, reflecting the pendulum-like swings of the shadow aspect of the personality (i.e., ego).

Fear of Abandonment Archetype
Versus
Fear of Engulfment Archetype

An individual holding over-riding fear of abandonment not atypically attracts and pairs with a person who holds overriding fear of engulfment. Initially, neither party to the pairing recognizes the abandonment/engulfment dynamic. But, at approximately 90 days into the relationship, the parties' shadows begin to reveal deeper aspects of their subconscious templates. At this juncture the couple may notice a pattern emerging in their interpersonal dynamic wherein one partner typically seems predominantly to pursue and the other seems predominantly to attempt to escape. This repetition of previously existing patterns creates the opportunity to heal these unresolved, unconscious patterns.

Anger/Dominant Archetype
Versus
Fear/Victim Archetype

An individual harboring over-riding anger/dominance traits frequently magnetically attracts a person who holds over-riding fear/victim tendencies. As the partners' shadows reveal themselves, one partner may reactively feel and express the pool of their unresolved anger while the other reactively feels and expresses victim tapes. Again, to evolve, to heal, we must reveal the buried stagnant emotions and thoughts. The pairing of opposites (anger/dominant archetype versus fear/victim archetype) creates the opportunity to heal these repetitive unresolved patterns. Did you ever notice how we can bounce from anger/controller to fearful/hopeless victim in an instant? The pendulum-like ego may shift from one archetype to another, in an uncentered individual.

Additional Personality Archetypes

When engaged in interpersonal dynamics with others, how do you react?

- **The Giver.** Here there is an imbalance in which one gives more than receives. The payayback is recognition by others of one's giving (which may well defeat the spirit of giving). Overly parental (maternal and/or paternal tendencies). Martyr. Innate need to be viewed as a hero.

- **The Blamer.** Initial inclination is to shift blame onto the other person.

- **The Intellectual.** Intellectualizes and rationalizes rather than feels pure emotion. Out of touch with the emotions (intellectualizes the emotions). Intellectuals think they are feeling, but this is merely thinking, not feeling.

- **The Escape Artist.** Avoids confrontation, at all costs.

- **The Balanced Congruent.** Minimal inappropriate reactivity, balanced response to conflict. Gives equal to receiving. Does not blame others; takes responsibility for contribution to a dynamic. Does not intellectualize emotion. Does not avoid confrontation.

Seven-Year Life-Lesson Cycle

Every seven years we enter a progressively advanced stage of evolutionary development. This happens at ages 14, 21, 28, 35, and so on. The worldly manifestations of these transitions reflect internal energetic development (of the chakras). As we near a transitional stage, we may find that life begins to shake and rattle a bit—i.e., we face healing crises (periods during which challenging circumstances prevail, for the purpose of helping us let go of beliefs—regarding people, objects, events—that no longer serve us). The reason? To help us master lessons and evolve. During these challenging transitions, life issues may seem accelerated and, sometimes, extreme. For example, we may face profound change that takes the form of profound life-changing decisions, including change of career path, and/or letting go of a spouse/mate, where the career path or relationship is not in our (and their) ultimate best interest. What is false will fall away during these profound transitional phases. The life cycle takes on the following approximate sequence. At age 14, the approximate onset of the teen-age years, we focus upon the emotions. During the teen-age years the highly-charged endocrine/hormone system sparks the emotions to full tilt. Transcription of emotional activity inspires endocrine activity to "attack" the internal organs. As such the emotions are stored biochemically via endocrine messengers within the internal organs. [See *Voice of the Soul: A Call to Action* for more.] The point is that we learn about the emotions during the seven-year period ranging from age 14 to age 21. At age 21, we shift our focus to intellectual activity. The period from age 21 to 28 typically contains intensified study gained through on-the-job training or graduate school. So, we spend the majority of our 20s honing our career skills.

In sum, we spend the pre-teenage years in the body and personality and initiate physical, emotional, and mental development. During the teenage years, the personality deals with emotions. During the 20s, the personality develops enhanced mental competence. Yet, a great transition occurs at approximately age 28 — when the prior dormant soul begins to speak up.

At approximately age 28, the soul begins to speak. Until this time, the personality has run the show. The personality has been free to experiment — emotionally, mentally, and spiritually. During this time, for the initial 28 years of living, the soul has remained relatively silent. The wise soul, who knows who we are, allows the personality to experiment freely — until age 28. At 28, the soul reviews the personality's beliefs and attachments (to people, objects, events, etc.). Wherever the personality's beliefs and attachments are not aligned with one's truth (as known by the soul) — the soul engages a mechanism whereby all attachments that are not soul-aligned (aligned with one's true life purpose and true life service) will begin to rattle and shake (i.e., issues shall arise), rattling and shaking with such strength until they ultimately fall away (or until the parties to the relationship learn and resolve issues between).

In other words, any interpersonal relationship (romance, work-related, family-related, friend-related, etc.) that is not aligned with one's truest path will develop challenging "issues," lessons to be learned. The parties will either learn and resolve the issues, or may learn and, given discernment, let go of the relationship. For example, if a career path or relationship is not appropriate for one's true path, serious issues will arise—and the result may be the change of career or the letting go of the relationship—unless resolution occurs and is aligned with each party's soul-aligned path. Sometimes it is in two people's best interest to resolve issues and continue their interactive dynamic. Yet, sometimes it's best for two people to resolve issues—and let go. It's a matter of discernment. The great question regards whether continuing a relational dynamic serves the highest interest (i.e., learning) for each person. Note that love is a lesson. As is commitment. The ultimate lesson may regard committing to one another. Learning how to love at a core level. Or the lesson may be regarding letting go. Lessons vary case by case. The soul knows the answers. Learn how to access the wisdom of the soul. [See *Voice of the Soul: A Call to Action*.]

A somewhat related concept is the seven-year itch. This may occur at any age but simply states that somehow we humans are wired so that we seem able to clearly discern situations given seven years of review. For example, you might stay with a career or relationship for seven years, after which something deep inside tells you that you've learned all you were meant to learn, cannot squeeze more love out of the situation, and it may be time to move on, or to go deeper inside, to another level of connection. At the seven-year juncture, we are forced to dig deeper—to go within, to listen to the whisper of intuition, and to follow its guidance. Note that the seven-year itch simply highlights seven-year cycles—but not cycles specific to a given age.

Chapter Six

LONGEVITY OF RELATIONSHIP

Relationship is Now (Not Past or Future)

LOVE BLOSSOMS FROM THE SOUL, NOT FROM EGO. Soul focuses only upon the present moment. Soul is not focused upon past or future moments. In contrast, ego is focused only on the (so-called) past and (so-called) future. Ego cannot access the present moment. And so (pure, real, unconditional) love is focused only in the now. *Love is an activity (of intention, words, or action) that occurs now*. And now. And now. In fact, any activity focused in the now — i.e., steeped in presence — is loving, by definition. As presence is love. As love resides only in the present moment. And as presence is accompanied only by love. The soul resides only in the present moment. Any activity aligned with the soul is loving. Soul-aligned activity [see *Voice of the Soul: A Call to Action*] brings us into the present moment. Presence is achieved only when one is engaged in activity born in the womb of the soul. The goal of relationship is to teach us how to love — in every moment. In other words, the goal of relationship is to teach us how to be present. Again, pure, true, unconditional love occurs only in the now. Not in so-called past or so-called future. And so, *pure relationship learns how to focus upon the present moment*. Pure relationship is presence — and pure love.

Love is a verb. The functional definition of love is any activity that supports another on their highest path in every moment. So a loving act is any act that helps another to align with his/her soul — i.e., to be wholly present in every moment. Love acts — silently, quietly, moderately, or loudly — in this moment. In this moment. In this moment. And so on. Acting selflessly to support the other person's highest interest, and acting self-lovingly to support one's own highest interest. A great paradox states that any activity that helps oneself or helps another in the greatest possible way, helps both parties (in the long-run). Love selflessly yet self-lovingly. It is not only possible, but essential, to do both, simultaneously.

A loving relationship, whether platonic or romantic, is focused in the present moment—while innately considering the long-term effect of any present action (as *right activity* inherently considers the long-term consequence of all present acts in all subsequent moments). A loving relationship is grounded by the presence (present moment focus) of the parties. [See *Voice of the Soul: A Call to Action*.]

Tests of Discernment

One specific system of healing holds that there are five fundamental emotions. These are given as anger, sadness, fear, joy, and doubt. The theory states that in the initial stages of healing, we humans find it difficult to separate feelings of pure anger from feelings of pure sadness. Rather, we experience feelings of anger and sadness bundled together in response to external stimuli, rather than experiencing feelings of pure emotion (pure anger and pure sadness experienced as distinctly separate emotions). Additionally, this system of healing states that during subsequent aspects of our healing, we must step through fear to access eventually the experience of joy. Finally, this system of healing proposes that doubt is everywhere—and that we will continually deal with feelings of doubt, until we achieve a profound state of evolution.

Doubt constantly tests us. And will continue to do so. Doubt challenges us. Doubt presents an opportunity to learn ... discernment. Doubt challenges our ability to discern between alternatives. This is the gift of doubt. The reward gained by facing doubt is an enhanced ability to make decisions—via enhanced discernment. In this, we consider what is best for ourselves and all other parties to any decision.

Like rats in a spinning wheel, we repeat lessons until we learn the lesson (i.e., resolve its underlying subconscious and conscious energies). However, even after we have released and healed former stagnant (unhealthy) subconscious and conscious patterns from deep within our energetic templates, doubt will still exist. Doubt is everywhere and ever shall be (again, until we achieve profound self-awareness/evolution). Yet, doubt is not a red light (stop signal). Rather, doubt is a green light—a signal that we must continue on our journey toward self-awareness. Through experience. Even after resolving an issue, prior-tempting bait may be waved before us, to tempt to veer from newly gained wisdom. Should we not take the bait, and continue to walk the new, more evolved, path—eventually our subconscious templates will cease to attract triggers, and mirrors, for the freshly-resolved issue. [See *Voice of the Soul: A Call to Action* for further explanation.] As an example, even after resolving a core issue, we still may attract a new partner who triggers the pattern of the former issue. This tests whether we react in the old way, or the new way. If we react (or non-react) in the new (more evolved) manner, we will stop attracting partners who test whether we've healed the issue.

True Power, Flow, Life-Stream, and the Natural Flow of Relationship

It is not the strongest species that survives.
Nor is it the most intelligent.
It is the species most adaptable to change that survives.
Inspired by Charles Darwin

In nature, flow is health. Non-flow is stagnancy, which leads to disease, which leads to death. We are born supple and die rigid. Inflexibility is the modus operandi of those who are disciples of death. To be soft and yielding is to promote vitality and longevity of life. She who is open to natural flow is vital. She who trusts her natural responses will find that all falls into place—as supported by natural order. She who wastes nothing experientially—i.e., she who is truly open to learning from *all* experience, whether judged as good or bad by the monkeymind (egoic aspect of personality)—is the epitome of healthful and complete living.

You are a river. A river of vital energy. A river fed by many streams of energy. Fed by the energy of the sun, the universe, the Earth. Danger lurks when we try to feed off of the energy of another person. Competition may be healthy or unhealthy. Unhealthy competition involves competitors who try to steal (finite, mortal) energy from one another, or attempt to block one another from receiving (infinite) energy from appropriate sources (sun, universe, and Earth). An example of unhealthy competition was the Tanya Harding/Nancy Kerrigan incident, in which an Olympic-caliber figure-skater, Tanya Harding, hired an associate to hurt the knee of another Olympic-caliber skater, Nancy Kerrigan. In effect, Tanya Harding attempted to isolate Nancy Kerrigan from fully utilizing her life-stream.

Only by living in our own **life-stream**, your natural flow — even when paired in relationship (platonic or romantic) may we experience the true self. Attempts to control (i.e., resist) natural flow are at the very least, futile, and, in the worst case, detrimental. If in harmony with natural flow, you cannot harmoniously control other people — or their life streams. The same is true for others not controlling you. We must live as integral beings while engaged in platonic or romantic relationship, or else the relationship will ultimately fail to achieve highest expression (highest learning, evolution and, if appropriate, longevity).

Love another completely — i.e., help partners to tap highest consciousness (infinite energy) — yet do not give them your personal (finite, mortal) energy. Does this make sense to you? Don't let anyone block your connection to highest consciousness. For only when we are connected to the Infinite (through soul-aligned activity) may we give fully and completely to another.

Interpersonal boundaries are askew (unaligned) or inappropriately entangled when we attempt to entwine our life stream with the life stream of another person, rather than living from the core and depth of our own life stream — as it connects to the infinite source of consciousness. As an example, co-dependence on the flow of another removes one from his/her life stream.

Longevity of Relationship

The relationship that lasts works through the interpersonal dynamic that preserves or enhances initial compatibility and maintains a high degree of shadow compatibility. Initial physical, mental, emotional, and/or spiritual attraction must persist as this is the glue to keep the parties sufficiently connected to choose to try to work out their interpersonal conflict. The couple must find a way to process and resolve issues *as a proactive team rather than as reactive adversaries* — employing effective communication that is based in love in all instances (rather than unawareness, misinterpretation, mistrust, and selfishness). A pairing with moderate initial compatibility (glue) may last, if appropriate, so long as there is substantial shadow-compatibility. A couple with minimal shadow-compatibility is less likely to experience longevity. Longevity is determined more by relative degree of shadow-compatibility (ability to resolve lessons presented in the form of conflictive issues between) than by degree of initial compatibility (nectar).

Relationships are designed to last for "a reason, a season, or a lifetime." The greater the degrees of initial compatibility and shadow compatibility, the greater the probability that the parties to the relationship will learn the lessons they are meant to learn from the pairing. The relationship may appropriately last a lifetime or a relatively brief period of time. The higher purpose of relationship is to learn about ourselves, through interaction with others. A relationship may last a lifetime given adequate initial compatibility, shadow compatibility, and if the parties to the relationship continue to learn lessons in a positive manner while in association with one another. A couple with great initial compatibility and shadow compatibility may decide to dissolve their association when fundamental and advanced lessons have been mastered. Yet, paradoxically, note that such a couple may choose to remain together indefinitely, as there are always lessons to be learned while in association with another — even if the lesson is simply peace and harmony — obviously an exquisite lesson — although, from the perspective of the soul, no more exquisite than any other lesson learned while relating to another (or others).

The Three Virtues

The *Tao Te Ching*, an ancient book of Chinese wisdom, states that the three great virtues are patience, compassion, and simplicity, as we mentioned earlier. It is essential that parties to a relationship maintain these virtues, both individually and with regard to one another. The practice of patience requires that you maintain faith in natural order — especially when most challenging to do so. Here, faith is the knowing that natural order will give you precisely what you need, when needed — from a universal, spiritual, and mostly subconscious perspective. Compassion requires the practice of forgiveness and understanding that the core of any person (soul) is wonderful, beautiful, and well-intended; compassion recognizes that the egoic aspect of any person is mortal and thereby still evolving — and thereby prone to making bad choices. Simplicity requires curbing desire to a degree of reasonableness and moderation.

The Coach (Referee)

In relationships where shadow compatibility is minimal (i.e., where the parties fail to embrace conflict as an essential springboard to evolution both individually and as a couple — and thereby experience profound miscommunication, growing mistrust, enhanced conflict, etc.), it may be prudent to invite a third-party to help facilitate open, honest, and helpful communication between the parties.

Chapter Seven

COUPLE ASSESSMENT

WHEN WORKING AS A HOLISTIC LIFE COACH (referee) with couples who experience ineffective and inefficient communication, I find that it is beneficial for each party to prepare four lists detailing complaints, recognized triggers, recognized mirroring and projection, and assumed responsibility. The parties do not share the lists with one another until the coach-referee has reviewed and assisted in editing the lists, removing inflammatory language/emotion/energy—so that the other party will be able to receive the information fully, without need for shielding against criticism or insult.

In these situations, the couple can be described as consisting of a person expressing complaints. In legal contexts, this person is termed the plaintiff (or complainer). If we see into these or any complaints, we may see solutions or resolutions, which are not always recognized or apparent in the complaint. This is why the plaintiff may also be called the petitioner. To complete the twosome, the person against whom these complaints are addressed, the defendant, is also the person being petitioned, the person who answers the petition, and so is also called the respondent. In our discussion here, perhaps the idea of asking for something, petitioning, is more helpful to much of our presentation and understanding.

Couple Self-Assessment Exercise—Lists of Complaints, Triggers, Mirrors/Projection and Responsibility

The lists are initially prepared individually by the petitioner, and then reviewed with the coach-referee. Then the lists are amended by these two. After thorough review and re-editing, the lists are shared between the coach-referee alone with the partner in the couple, here considered as the respondent.

The initial list prepared by petitioners regards unilateral complaints about interaction with their partners, the respondents. Following review of the complaint list with the coach-referee, a list of triggers, mirrors, and projections is prepared; this list describes what is really happening (in the professional opinion of the coach-referee). Finally, a list pinpointing the responsibility of the complaint or request (petition) directed at the respondents is created by petitioners and thereafter reviewed by the referee. (In this responsibility list, the petitioners explain how they contributed to the situation—in essence placing "blame" upon themselves, rather than the partner. (Note that in extreme examples, where physical abuse is evident, the plaintiffs/victims of abuse are self-responsible to the extent that they chose this relationship and chose to stay—up to this juncture. The lesson therein is discernment - knowing it's time to leave.)

The coach-referee then shares these lists alone with each respondent. Finally, the referee reviews all lists with the couple *together*. Note that by the time the couple reviews their lists together, each has previously seen both lists and has learned how they are responsible for the conflict and miscommunication. This serves to minimize the risk of surprise and spontaneous adverse reaction when truth is shared with both parties present.

Once there is a resolution of the lessons considered, the couple will likely understand whether remaining together, to engage in further lessons, is appropriate or not.

Conclusion

WORLD LEADERS, BUSINESS PARTNERS, FAMILY members, friends, lovers, and any other participants to any interpersonal dynamic are meant to evolve—through resolution of conflict. From a universal perspective, this is the express reason that conflict exists: to help us grow, to help us learn about ourselves—through others. At a subconscious level, we evolve by healing buried wounds of the past—by "unburying" the feelings we weren't yet ready to resolve. In other words we must refill, feel again, the emotions we buried long before, to move forward (i.e., evolve).

To refeel buried emotions, to again experience similar emotions, so we can finally heal the emotion, we must be triggered to refeel through through relationship with another person. Other people "push our buttons" (i.e., trigger us to feel and refeel) — by universal design ... which provides opportunities for their growth and ours.

No parties to any conflict are so far apart on any issues — excluding abusive situations — not to be able to resolve the challenging lessons. We can remember that the outcome of resolution may not be harmonious, peaceful, or lasting; true resolution concerns resolution of unresolved internal energies (emotions, etc.), but not necessarily resolution of the superficial aspects of the conflict. Thus, the parties may ultimately simply agree to disagree ... and move on, individually.

And so the parties to a dynamic are necessarily meant to stay together indefinitely; this may not be the case. Thus, a relationship may run its course in a season rather than a lifetime — if the parties no longer learn valuable lessons from interaction with one another. Yet, given a sincere and systematic attempt to resolve an interpersonal issue, each individual evolves — at least a bit — easing communication and understanding in the current dynamic, or in subsequent interpersonal dynamics.

Given a committed attempt to resolve an issue, eventually the best course of action becomes visible and obvious to both parties of the relationship — whether to stay together or to let the attachment go, and to open to the possibility of new connections.

In my experience I have found that whenever individuals commit to such a process of healing, resolution of issues culminates in greater mutual understanding, self-awareness, respect, compassion, patience, and intimacy — be it in the current relationship or in subsequent relationships.

Additionally, given resolution of an issue, we obviously no longer need to deal with this issue in a current relationship. In this case, we can watch the relationship grow and become more profound. Here, in the growing current relationship, we may be addressing other, relatively advanced, issues. Or, if it becomes clear that it's appropriate to move on, these further, potentially deeper, issues may arise in a new relationship that we then open ourselves to.

In theory, any two people can find a way to resolve conflict and grow together, given mutual commitment to systematic evolution.

Addendum

ATTRACTING and SELECTING AN APPROPRIATE LIFE PARTNER — An Eastern Perspective

THE WESTERN PARADIGM FOR SELECTION OF A MATE, in its most stereotypical form, is gender-specific. Women in traditionally-stereotypical relationships sought male partners who were competent as provider, companion, and protector; a less important quality sought by women in traditionally-stereotypical relationships regarded a man's spiritual sensibilities. Men in traditionally-stereotypical relationships sought female partners who held obvious aesthetic beauty, who were competent as companions, and who supported the male's vision and life-stream (i.e., a "socially-presentable" woman if coupled with a materially-focused male, a "good mother" if paired with a family-oriented male, etc.). Whereas these qualities and subjective selections are not inappropriate, per se, the list seems *superficial* (materially-oriented) relative to values innate to ancient Eastern and indigenous cultures.

In the sacred writings of ancient cultures, *consciousness* is described in masculine terms (as masculine energy), and *power* is identified with feminine energy. In Hindu terms, the Universe was created by the Dance of Shiva, masculine energy, and was ignited and powered by the feminine energy of Shakti. Shiva is considered a sleeping, dormant male consciousness (within ourselves) that must be awakened by the dynamic power of female energy (within ourselves). Note that relationship is not a requisite for the melding of female and male energies, as each individual holds both female and male energy—and may create unity of these forces within onself. Yet, with regard to interpersonal relationship, the Eastern paradigm values the female partner for her true power—not based in seductive or manipulative power, but rather as a giving energy that is sourced by the eternal, infinite pool of consciousness; such giving does not sacrifice one's own finite, mortal energy. The Eastern paradigm values the male partner for his higher aspect, his ideals.

To manifest an appropriate partner, do your work. Align with the soul [see *Voice of the Soul: A Call to Action*] as energy magnetically attracts like-energy. If you've healed many wounds, you will attract a partner with similarly healed energy, such that you both may help (trigger) one another to learn and resolve progressively advanced (i.e., subtle) lessons.

After you have attracted a potential partner, you may (or may not) gain subtle (or not-so-subtle) hints regarding possible lessons to be learned through the interpersonal dynamic based upon:

- **Analyses of personality archetypes** that consider each participants' historical patterns of dynamic (i.e., prior engulfment versus abandonment issues, dominator versus victim issues, etc.);

- **Numerology** (birth number, etc.);

- **Astrology** (birth time and place—but only given a complete astrological chart analysis by a credible astrologer ... don't simply consider the "sun sign");

- **Birth order** (eldest children statistically relate best to younger children—unless the youngest is much younger than siblings, in which case this child behaves like an eldest child in interpersonal dynamics);

- **Core creativity aspect** (dancer, musician or visual artist: birth/core artists mimic "air-character" traits, birth/core dancers mimic "earth-character" traits, and birth/core musicians mimic a less discernible combination of "element-character" trait; and

- **Better yet, ignore the preceding analytical methods** — as they are subjective (i.e., don't reveal absolutely clear information) — and simply remain present in each moment, give it your best shot, and observe patterns of the dynamic — without pre-conceived notions of how things should proceed based upon subjective theory.

How to Heal a Relationship (and the Self)

We are holistic beings. What does "holistic" mean? It means that body and mind are entwined to such extent that to heal one you must heal the other. In other words, we must heal both body and mind to experience sustained healing. How do we heal mind? Talk to a therapist, read a book, etc. And why must we heal the body? As the ancient Taoists believed, the emotions are biochemically/bioenergetically stored in the internal organs. To release stagnant (unhealthy) energy, we may engage in conscious activities, including conscious creativity, which is centered upon real-time emotion. [For more detail, see *Voice of the Soul: A Call to Action*.]

Approach Relational Issues as Pro-Active Allies — Not Reactive Adversaries!

If the parties to any relationship proactively recognize that they most certainly will experience relational issues at some juncture (with subtle or not-so-subtle hints likely beginning at approximately 90 days into the dynamic), and that these issues are an essential part of the dynamic — by universal design (to help one another to evolve), then it may be easier for the parties to approach one another with the open communication of allies—rather than the closed-hearted discourse of reactive adversaries, who react after-the-fact to triggered conflict—more so as they do not accept and thereby embrace conflict between them as an essential aspect of the relationship.

So at this point, we can imagine these two options: being in a relationship where we act as a reactive adversary to our partner, where we act as an ally with our partner; which is more appealing? Higher vision invites us to the second!

ABOUT THE AUTHOR

Andrew Sadock resides in Chicago, Los Angeles, and northeastern Michigan. During summers, he serves as owner and captain of an authentic wooden tall ship, *Red Witch*, a 77-foot, 41-ton wooden two-masted gaff-rigged schooner. (See redwitch.com.) During winters, Mr. Sadock serves as a holistic life coach/consultant, energyworker, qi gong instructor, motivational speaker, and performing musician; he also offers silent meditation sails—featuring whale and dolphin sightings—on the Pacific Ocean from Marina Del Rey.

Mr. Sadock has the intention to serve as a professor to introduce a curriculum of holistic philosophy/psychology/energetic medicine to universities adapted from three books he has authored that comprise the Anatomy of the Human Fabric Trilogy. Additionally, he intends to create a non-profit foundation to serve underprivileged children aboard his tall ship and sailboat (in Chicago and Los Angeles).

He practiced holistic energywork and bodywork in Chicago, San Francisco, and at Esalen Institute (Big Sur). He has written this series of three books—*Anatomy of the Human Fabric Trilogy*—on holistic philosophy/psychology/energetics. Mr. Sadock also created a screenplay adaptation of the first book he wrote, which chronicles a profound true tale of synchronicity (chronicling an inadvertent shift from medical school to a decade-long residence, meditation, and journey with shamans/indigenous healers, and the eventual practice of holistic medicine/psychology/energetics).

Mr. Sadock's background includes experience as an energyworker, certified qi gong teacher, licensed massage therapist, child advocate, musician (composer, lyricist, guitarist, sitarist, vocalist), U.S. Merchant Marine Officer (100-ton qualification), sailor, motorcyclist, rugby player, and rugby coach. (See deadsea7.com.)

In addition to the above three books and screenplay, Mr. Sadock has created two CDs, *Yang* (world percussive jazz) and *Yin* (contemplative ambient), designed to enhance inner vibration.

CONTACT INFORMATION

Email: asadock@gmail.com
URL: AndrewSadock.com

www.ingramcontent.com/pod-product-compliance
Lightning Source LLC
LaVergne TN
LVHW091319080426
835510LV00007B/556